President Trump's Revised Executive Order on Travel

Compiled by
Feddie E.O

Copyrighted Material

Copyright ©2017 by Feddie E.O

ISBN- 13: 978-1544631998

All rights reversed.

No part of this publication maybe reproduced, stored in retrieval system, or transmitted in any form or by any means, electronic, mechanical, photocopying, recording or otherwise without the prior written permission of the editor or publisher (Createspace publishing resources).

Contact:
Website : www.createspace.com

Contents

Introduction   4

Executive Order 13780—Protecting The Nation From Foreign Terrorist Entry Into The United States   5

Executive Order 13769—Protecting The Nation From Foreign Terrorist Entry Into The United States   20

Memorandum on Implementing Immediate Heightened Screening and Vetting of Applications for Visas and Other Immigration Benefits March 6, 2017   28

Introduction

The entry into the United States of foreign nationals who may commit, aid, or support acts of terrorism remains a matter of grave concern to President Trump. In light of the Ninth Circuit's observation that the political branches are better suited to determine the appropriate scope of any suspensions than are the courts, and in order to avoid spending additional time pursuing litigation, Trump revoking Executive Order 13769 and replacing it with this order, which expressly excludes from the suspensions categories of aliens that have prompted judicial concerns and which clarifies or refines the approach to certain other issues or categories of affected aliens.

Executive Order Protecting The Nation From Foreign Terrorist Entry Into The United States

EXECUTIVE ORDER = (REVESRED TRAVEL BAN)

- - - - - - -

PROTECTING THE NATION FROM FOREIGN TERRORIST ENTRY INTO THE UNITED STATES

By the authority vested in me as President by the Constitution and the laws of the United States of America, including the Immigration and Nationality Act (INA), 8 U.S.C. 1101 et seq., and section 301 of title 3, United States Code, and to protect the Nation from terrorist activities by foreign nationals admitted to the United States, it is hereby ordered as follows:

Section 1. Policy and Purpose. (a) It is the policy of the United States to protect its citizens from terrorist attacks, including those committed by foreign nationals. The screening and vetting protocols and procedures associated with the visa-issuance process and the United States Refugee Admissions Program (USRAP) play a crucial role in detecting foreign nationals who may commit, aid, or support acts of terrorism and in preventing those individuals from entering the United States. It is therefore the policy of the United States to improve the screening and vetting protocols and procedures associated with the visa-issuance process and the USRAP.

(b) On January 27, 2017, to implement this policy, I issued Executive Order 13769 (Protecting the Nation from Foreign Terrorist Entry into the United States).

(i) Among other actions, Executive Order 13769 suspended for 90 days the entry of certain aliens from seven countries: Iran, Iraq, Libya, Somalia, Sudan, Syria, and Yemen. These are countries that had already been identified as presenting heightened concerns about terrorism and travel to the United States. Specifically, the suspension applied to countries referred to in, or designated under, section 217(a)(12) of the INA, 8 U.S.C. 1187(a)(12), in which Congress restricted use of the Visa Waiver Program for nationals of, and aliens recently present in, (A) Iraq or Syria, (B) any country designated by the Secretary of State as a state sponsor of terrorism (currently Iran, Syria, and Sudan), and (C) any other country designated as a country of concern by the Secretary of Homeland Security, in consultation with the Secretary of State and the Director of National Intelligence. In 2016, the Secretary of Homeland Security designated Libya, Somalia, and Yemen as additional countries of concern for travel purposes, based on consideration of three statutory factors related to terrorism and national security: "(I) whether the presence of an alien in the country or area increases the likelihood that the alien is a credible threat to the national security of the United States; (II) whether a foreign terrorist organization has a significant presence in the country or area; and (III) whether the country or area is a safe haven for terrorists." 8 U.S.C. 1187(a)(12)(D)(ii). Additionally, Members of Congress have expressed concerns about screening and vetting procedures following recent terrorist attacks in this country and in Europe.

(ii) In ordering the temporary suspension of entry described in subsection (b)(i) of this section, I exercised my authority under Article II of the Constitution and under section 212(f) of the INA, which provides in relevant part: "Whenever the President finds that the entry of any aliens or of any class of aliens into the United States would be detrimental to the interests of the United States, he may by proclamation, and for such period as he shall deem necessary, suspend the entry of all aliens or any class of aliens as immigrants or nonimmigrants, or impose on the entry of aliens any restrictions he may deem to be appropriate." 8 U.S.C. 1182(f). Under these authorities, I determined that, for a brief period of 90 days, while existing screening and vetting procedures were under review, the entry into the United States of certain aliens from the seven identified countries -- each afflicted by terrorism in a manner that compromised the ability of the United States to rely on normal decision-making procedures about travel to the United States -- would be detrimental to the interests of the United States. Nonetheless, I permitted the Secretary of State and the Secretary of Homeland Security to grant case-by-case waivers when they determined that it was in the national interest to do so.

(iii) Executive Order 13769 also suspended the USRAP for 120 days. Terrorist groups have sought to infiltrate several nations through refugee programs. Accordingly, I temporarily suspended the USRAP pending a review of our procedures for screening and vetting refugees. Nonetheless, I permitted the Secretary of State and the Secretary of Homeland Security to jointly grant case-by-case waivers when they determined that it was in the national interest to do so.

(iv) Executive Order 13769 did not provide a basis for discriminating for or against members of any particular religion. While that order allowed for prioritization of refugee claims from members of persecuted religious minority groups, that priority applied to refugees from every nation, including those in which Islam is a minority religion, and it applied to minority sects within a religion. That order was not motivated by animus toward any religion, but was instead intended to protect the ability of religious minorities -- whoever they are and wherever they reside -- to avail themselves of the USRAP in light of their particular challenges and circumstances.

(c) The implementation of Executive Order 13769 has been delayed by litigation. Most significantly, enforcement of critical provisions of that order has been temporarily halted by court orders that apply nationwide and extend even to foreign nationals with no prior or substantial connection to the United States. On February 9, 2017, the United States Court of Appeals for the Ninth Circuit declined to stay or narrow one such order pending the outcome of further judicial proceedings, while noting that the "political branches are far better equipped to make appropriate distinctions" about who should be covered by a suspension of entry or of refugee admissions.

(d) Nationals from the countries previously identified under section 217(a)(12) of the INA warrant additional scrutiny in connection with our immigration policies because the conditions in these countries present heightened threats. Each of these countries is a state sponsor of terrorism, has been significantly compromised by terrorist organizations, or contains active conflict zones. Any of these circumstances diminishes the foreign government's willingness or ability to share or validate important information about individuals seeking to travel to the United States. Moreover, the significant presence in each of these countries of terrorist organizations, their members, and others exposed to those organizations increases the chance that conditions will be exploited to enable terrorist operatives or sympathizers to travel to the United States. Finally, once foreign nationals from these countries are admitted to the United States, it is often difficult to remove them, because many of these countries typically delay issuing, or refuse to issue, travel documents.

(e) The following are brief descriptions, taken in part from the Department of State's Country Reports on Terrorism 2015 (June 2016), of some of the conditions in six of the previously designated countries that demonstrate why their nationals continue to present heightened risks to the security of the United States:

(i) Iran. Iran has been designated as a state sponsor of terrorism since 1984 and continues to support various terrorist groups, including Hizballah, Hamas, and terrorist groups in Iraq. Iran has also been linked to support for al-Qa'ida and has permitted al-Qa'ida to transport funds and fighters through Iran to Syria and South Asia. Iran does not cooperate with the United States in counterterrorism efforts.

(ii) Libya. Libya is an active combat zone, with hostilities between the internationally recognized government and its rivals. In many parts of the country, security and law enforcement functions are provided by armed militias rather than state institutions. Violent extremist groups, including the Islamic State of Iraq and Syria (ISIS), have exploited these conditions to expand their presence in the country. The Libyan government provides some cooperation with the United States' counterterrorism efforts, but it is unable to secure thousands of miles of its land and maritime borders, enabling the illicit flow of weapons, migrants, and foreign terrorist fighters. The United States Embassy in Libya suspended its operations in 2014.

(iii) Somalia. Portions of Somalia have been terrorist safe havens. Al-Shabaab, an al-Qa'ida-affiliated terrorist group, has operated in the country for years and continues to plan and mount operations within Somalia and in neighboring countries. Somalia has porous borders, and most countries do not recognize Somali identity documents. The Somali government cooperates with the United States in some counterterrorism operations but does not have the capacity to sustain military pressure on or to investigate suspected terrorists.

(iv) Sudan. Sudan has been designated as a state sponsor of terrorism since 1993 because of its support for international terrorist groups, including Hizballah and Hamas. Historically, Sudan provided safe havens for al-Qa'ida and other terrorist groups to meet and train. Although Sudan's support to al-Qa'ida has ceased and it provides some cooperation with the United States' counterterrorism efforts, elements of core al-Qa'ida and ISIS-linked terrorist groups remain active in the country.

(v) Syria. Syria has been designated as a state sponsor of terrorism since 1979. The Syrian government is engaged in an ongoing military conflict against ISIS and others for control of portions of the country. At the same time, Syria continues to support other terrorist groups. It has allowed or encouraged extremists to pass through its territory to enter Iraq. ISIS continues to attract foreign fighters to Syria and to use its base in Syria to plot or encourage attacks around the globe, including in the United States. The United States Embassy in Syria suspended its operations in 2012. Syria does not cooperate with the United States' counterterrorism efforts.

(vi) Yemen. Yemen is the site of an ongoing conflict between the incumbent government and the Houthi-led opposition. Both ISIS and a second group, al-Qa'ida in the Arabian Peninsula (AQAP), have exploited this conflict to expand their presence in Yemen and to carry out hundreds of attacks. Weapons and other materials smuggled across Yemen's porous borders are used to finance AQAP and other terrorist activities. In 2015, the United States Embassy in Yemen suspended its operations, and embassy staff were relocated out of the country. Yemen has been supportive of, but has not been able to cooperate fully with, the United States in counterterrorism efforts.

(f) In light of the conditions in these six countries, until the assessment of current screening and vetting procedures required by section 2 of this order is completed, the risk of erroneously permitting entry of a national of one of these countries who intends to commit terrorist acts or otherwise harm the national security of the United States is unacceptably high. Accordingly, while that assessment is ongoing, I am imposing a temporary pause on the entry of nationals from Iran, Libya, Somalia, Sudan, Syria, and Yemen, subject to categorical exceptions and case-by-case waivers, as described in section 3 of this order.

(g) Iraq presents a special case. Portions of Iraq remain active combat zones. Since 2014, ISIS has had dominant influence over significant territory in northern and central Iraq. Although that influence has been significantly reduced due to the efforts and sacrifices of the Iraqi government and armed forces, working along with a United States-led coalition, the ongoing conflict has impacted the Iraqi government's capacity to secure its borders and to identify fraudulent travel documents. Nevertheless, the close cooperative relationship between the United States and the democratically elected Iraqi government, the strong United States diplomatic presence in Iraq, the significant presence of United States forces in Iraq, and Iraq's commitment to combat ISIS justify different treatment for Iraq. In particular, those Iraqi government forces that have fought to regain more than half of the territory previously dominated by ISIS have shown steadfast determination and earned enduring respect as they battle an armed group that is the common enemy of Iraq and the United States. In addition, since Executive Order 13769 was issued, the Iraqi government has expressly undertaken steps to enhance travel documentation, information sharing, and the return of Iraqi nationals subject to final orders of removal. Decisions about issuance of visas or granting admission to Iraqi nationals should be subjected to additional scrutiny to determine if applicants have connections with ISIS or other terrorist organizations, or otherwise pose a risk to either national security or public safety.

(h) Recent history shows that some of those who have entered the United States through our immigration system have proved to be threats to our national security. Since 2001, hundreds of persons born abroad have been convicted of terrorism-related crimes in the United States. They have included not just persons who came here legally on visas but also individuals who first entered the country as refugees. For example, in January 2013, two Iraqi nationals admitted to the United States as refugees in 2009 were sentenced to 40 years and to life in prison, respectively, for multiple terrorism-related offenses. And in October 2014, a native of Somalia who had been brought to the United States as a child refugee and later became a naturalized United States citizen was sentenced to 30 years in prison for attempting to use a weapon of mass destruction as part of a plot to detonate a bomb at a crowded Christmas-tree-lighting ceremony in Portland, Oregon. The Attorney General has reported to me that more than 300 persons who entered the United States as refugees are currently the subjects of counterterrorism investigations by the Federal Bureau of Investigation.

(i) Given the foregoing, the entry into the United States of foreign nationals who may commit, aid, or support acts of terrorism remains a matter of grave concern. In light of the Ninth Circuit's observation that the political branches are better suited to determine the appropriate scope of any suspensions than are the courts, and in order to avoid spending additional time pursuing litigation, I am revoking Executive Order 13769 and replacing it with this order, which expressly excludes from the suspensions categories of aliens that have prompted judicial concerns and which clarifies or refines the approach to certain other issues or categories of affected aliens.

Sec. 2. Temporary Suspension of Entry for Nationals of Countries of Particular Concern During Review Period. (a) The Secretary of Homeland Security, in consultation with the Secretary of State and the Director of National Intelligence, shall conduct a worldwide review to identify whether, and if so what, additional information will be needed from each foreign country to adjudicate an application by a national of that country for a visa, admission, or other benefit under the INA (adjudications) in order to determine that the individual is not a security or public-safety threat. The Secretary of Homeland Security may conclude that certain information is needed from particular countries even if it is not needed from every country.

(b) The Secretary of Homeland Security, in consultation with the Secretary of State and the Director of National Intelligence, shall submit to the President a report on the results of the worldwide review described in subsection (a) of this section, including the Secretary of Homeland Security's determination of the information needed from each country for adjudications and a list of countries that do not provide adequate information, within 20 days of the effective date of this order. The Secretary of Homeland Security shall provide a copy of the report to the Secretary of State, the Attorney General, and the Director of National Intelligence.

(c) To temporarily reduce investigative burdens on relevant agencies during the review period described in subsection (a) of this section, to ensure the proper review and maximum utilization of available resources for the screening and vetting of foreign nationals, to ensure that adequate standards are established to prevent infiltration by foreign terrorists, and in light of the national security concerns referenced in section 1 of this order, I hereby proclaim, pursuant to sections 212(f) and 215(a) of the INA, 8 U.S.C. 1182(f) and 1185(a), that the unrestricted entry into the United States of nationals of Iran, Libya, Somalia,

Sudan, Syria, and Yemen would be detrimental to the interests of the United States. I therefore direct that the entry into the United States of nationals of those six countries be suspended for 90 days from the effective date of this order, subject to the limitations, waivers, and exceptions set forth in sections 3 and 12 of this order.

(d) Upon submission of the report described in subsection (b) of this section regarding the information needed from each country for adjudications, the Secretary of State shall request that all foreign governments that do not supply such information regarding their nationals begin providing it within 50 days of notification.

(e) After the period described in subsection (d) of this section expires, the Secretary of Homeland Security, in consultation with the Secretary of State and the Attorney General, shall submit to the President a list of countries recommended for inclusion in a Presidential proclamation that would prohibit the entry of appropriate categories of foreign nationals of countries that have not provided the information requested until they do so or until the Secretary of Homeland Security certifies that the country has an adequate plan to do so, or has adequately shared information through other means. The Secretary of State, the Attorney General, or the Secretary of Homeland Security may also submit to the President the names of additional countries for which any of them recommends other lawful restrictions or limitations deemed necessary for the security or welfare of the United States.

(f) At any point after the submission of the list described in subsection (e) of this section, the Secretary of Homeland Security, in consultation with the Secretary of State and the Attorney General, may submit to the President the names of any additional countries recommended for similar treatment, as well as the names of any countries that they recommend should be removed from the scope of a proclamation described in subsection (e) of this section.

(g) The Secretary of State and the Secretary of Homeland Security shall submit to the President a joint report on the progress in implementing this order within 60 days of the effective date of this order, a second report within 90 days of the effective date of this order, a third report within 120 days of the effective date of this order, and a fourth report within 150 days of the effective date of this order.

Sec. 3. Scope and Implementation of Suspension.

(a) Scope. Subject to the exceptions set forth in subsection (b) of this section and any waiver under subsection (c) of this section, the suspension of entry pursuant to section 2 of this order shall apply only to foreign nationals of the designated countries who:

(i) are outside the United States on the effective date of this order;

(ii) did not have a valid visa at 5:00 p.m., eastern standard time on January 27, 2017; and

(iii) do not have a valid visa on the effective date of this order.

(b) Exceptions. The suspension of entry pursuant to section 2 of this order shall not apply to:

(i) any lawful permanent resident of the United States;

(ii) any foreign national who is admitted to or paroled into the United States on or after the effective date of this order;

(iii) any foreign national who has a document other than a visa, valid on the effective date of this order or issued on any date thereafter, that permits him or her to travel to the United States and seek entry or admission, such as an advance parole document;

(iv) any dual national of a country designated under section 2 of this order when the individual is traveling on a passport issued by a non-designated country;

(v) any foreign national traveling on a diplomatic or diplomatic-type visa, North Atlantic Treaty Organization visa, C-2 visa for travel to the United Nations, or G-1, G-2, G-3, or G-4 visa; or

(vi) any foreign national who has been granted asylum; any refugee who has already been admitted to the United States; or any individual who has been granted withholding of removal, advance parole, or protection under the Convention Against Torture.

(c) Waivers. Notwithstanding the suspension of entry pursuant to section 2 of this order, a consular officer, or, as appropriate, the Commissioner, U.S. Customs and Border Protection (CBP), or the Commissioner's delegee, may, in the consular officer's or the CBP official's discretion, decide on a case-by-case basis to authorize the issuance of a visa to, or to permit the entry of, a foreign national for whom entry is otherwise suspended if the foreign national has demonstrated to the officer's satisfaction that denying entry during the suspension period would cause undue hardship, and that his or her entry would not pose a threat to national security and would be in the national interest. Unless otherwise specified by the Secretary of Homeland Security, any waiver issued by a consular officer as part of the visa issuance process will be effective both for the issuance of a visa and any subsequent entry on that visa, but will leave all other requirements for admission or entry unchanged. Case-by-case waivers could be appropriate in circumstances such as the following:

(i) the foreign national has previously been admitted to the United States for a continuous period of work, study, or other long-term activity, is outside the United States on the effective date of this order, seeks to reenter the United States to resume that activity, and the denial of reentry during the suspension period would impair that activity;

(ii) the foreign national has previously established significant contacts with the United States but is outside the United States on the effective date of this order for work, study, or other lawful activity;

(iii) the foreign national seeks to enter the United States for significant business or professional obligations and the denial of entry during the suspension period would impair those obligations;

(iv) the foreign national seeks to enter the United States to visit or reside with a close family member (e.g., a spouse, child, or parent) who is a United States citizen, lawful permanent resident, or alien lawfully admitted on a valid nonimmigrant visa, and the denial of entry during the suspension period would cause undue hardship;

(v) the foreign national is an infant, a young child or adoptee, an individual needing urgent medical care, or someone whose entry is otherwise justified by the special circumstances of the case;

(vi) the foreign national has been employed by, or on behalf of, the United States Government (or is an eligible dependent of such an employee) and the employee can document that he or she has provided faithful and valuable service to the United States Government;

(vii) the foreign national is traveling for purposes related to an international organization designated under the International Organizations Immunities Act (IOIA), 22 U.S.C. 288 et seq., traveling for purposes of conducting meetings or business with the United States Government, or traveling to conduct business on behalf of an international organization not designated under the IOIA;

(viii) the foreign national is a landed Canadian immigrant who applies for a visa at a location within Canada; or

(ix) the foreign national is traveling as a United States Government-sponsored exchange visitor.

Sec. 4. Additional Inquiries Related to Nationals of Iraq. An application by any Iraqi national for a visa, admission, or other immigration benefit should be subjected to thorough review, including, as appropriate, consultation with a designee of the Secretary of Defense and use of the additional information that has been obtained in the context of the close U.S.-Iraqi security partnership, since Executive Order 13769 was issued, concerning individuals suspected of ties to ISIS or other terrorist organizations and individuals coming from territories controlled or formerly controlled by ISIS. Such review shall include consideration of whether the applicant has connections with ISIS or other terrorist organizations or with territory that is or has been under the dominant influence of ISIS, as well as any other information bearing on whether the applicant may be a threat to commit acts of terrorism or otherwise threaten the national security or public safety of the United States.

Sec. 5. Implementing Uniform Screening and Vetting Standards for All Immigration Programs. (a) The Secretary of State, the Attorney General, the Secretary of Homeland Security, and the Director of National Intelligence shall implement a program, as part of the process for adjudications, to identify individuals who seek to enter the United States on a fraudulent basis, who support terrorism, violent extremism, acts of violence toward any group or class of people within the United States, or who present a risk of causing harm subsequent to their entry. This program shall include the development of a uniform baseline for screening and vetting standards and procedures, such as in-person interviews; a database of identity documents proffered by applicants to ensure that duplicate documents are not used by multiple applicants; amended application forms that include questions aimed at identifying fraudulent answers and malicious intent; a mechanism to ensure that applicants are who they claim to be; a mechanism to assess whether applicants may commit, aid, or support any kind of violent, criminal, or terrorist acts after entering the United States; and any other appropriate means for ensuring the proper collection of all information necessary for a rigorous evaluation of all grounds of inadmissibility or grounds for the denial of other immigration benefits.

(b) The Secretary of Homeland Security, in conjunction with the Secretary of State, the Attorney General, and the Director of National Intelligence, shall submit to the President an initial report on the progress of the program described in subsection (a) of this section within 60 days of the effective date of this order, a second report within 100 days of the effective date of this order, and a third report within 200 days of the effective date of this order.

Sec. 6. Realignment of the U.S. Refugee Admissions Program for Fiscal Year 2017. (a) The Secretary of State shall suspend travel of refugees into the United States under the USRAP, and the Secretary of Homeland Security shall suspend decisions on applications for refugee status, for 120 days after the effective date of this order, subject to waivers pursuant to subsection (c) of this section. During the 120-day period, the Secretary of State, in conjunction with the Secretary of Homeland Security and in consultation with the Director of National Intelligence, shall review the USRAP application and adjudication processes to determine what additional procedures should be used to ensure that individuals seeking admission as refugees do not pose a threat to the security and welfare of the United States, and shall implement such additional procedures. The suspension described in this subsection shall not apply to refugee applicants who, before the effective date of this order, have been formally scheduled for transit by the Department of State. The Secretary of State shall resume travel of refugees into the United States under the USRAP 120 days after the effective date of this order, and the Secretary of Homeland Security shall resume making decisions on applications for refugee status only for stateless persons and nationals of countries for which the Secretary of State, the Secretary of Homeland Security, and the Director of National Intelligence have jointly determined that the additional procedures implemented pursuant to this subsection are adequate to ensure the security and welfare of the United States.

(b) Pursuant to section 212(f) of the INA, I hereby proclaim that the entry of more than 50,000 refugees in fiscal year 2017 would be detrimental to the interests of the United States, and thus suspend any entries in excess of that number until such time as I determine that additional entries would be in the national interest.

(c) Notwithstanding the temporary suspension imposed pursuant to subsection (a) of this section, the Secretary of State and the Secretary of Homeland Security may jointly determine to admit individuals to the United States as refugees on a case-by-case basis, in their discretion, but only so long as they determine that the entry of such individuals as refugees is in the national interest and does not pose a threat to the security or welfare of the United States, including in circumstances such as the following: the individual's entry would enable the United States to conform its conduct to a preexisting international agreement or arrangement, or the denial of entry would cause undue hardship.

(d) It is the policy of the executive branch that, to the extent permitted by law and as practicable, State and local jurisdictions be granted a role in the process of determining the placement or settlement in their jurisdictions of aliens eligible to be admitted to the United States as refugees. To that end, the Secretary of State shall examine existing law to determine the extent to which, consistent with applicable law, State and local jurisdictions may have greater involvement in the process of determining the placement or resettlement of refugees in their jurisdictions, and shall devise a proposal to lawfully promote such involvement.

Sec. 7. Rescission of Exercise of Authority Relating to the Terrorism Grounds of Inadmissibility. The Secretary of State and the Secretary of Homeland Security shall, in consultation with the Attorney General, consider rescinding the exercises of authority permitted by section 212(d)(3)(B) of the INA, 8 U.S.C. 1182(d)(3)(B), relating to the terrorism grounds of inadmissibility, as well as any related implementing directives or guidance.

Sec. 8. Expedited Completion of the Biometric Entry-Exit Tracking System. (a) The Secretary of Homeland Security shall expedite the completion and implementation of a biometric entry exit tracking system for in-scope travelers to the United States, as recommended by the National Commission on Terrorist Attacks Upon the United States.

(b) The Secretary of Homeland Security shall submit to the President periodic reports on the progress of the directive set forth in subsection (a) of this section. The initial report shall be submitted within 100 days of the effective date of this order, a second report shall be submitted within 200 days of the effective date of this order, and a third report shall be submitted within 365 days of the effective date of this order. The Secretary of Homeland Security shall submit further reports every 180 days thereafter until the system is fully deployed and operational.

Sec. 9. Visa Interview Security. (a) The Secretary of State shall immediately suspend the Visa Interview Waiver Program and ensure compliance with section 222 of the INA, 8 U.S.C. 1202, which requires that all individuals seeking a nonimmigrant visa undergo an in-person interview, subject to specific statutory exceptions. This suspension shall not apply to any foreign national traveling on a diplomatic or diplomatic-type visa, North Atlantic Treaty Organization visa, C-2 visa for travel to the United Nations, or G-1, G-2, G-3, or G-4 visa; traveling for purposes related to an international organization designated under the IOIA; or traveling for purposes of conducting meetings or business with the United States Government.

(b) To the extent permitted by law and subject to the availability of appropriations, the Secretary of State shall immediately expand the Consular Fellows Program, including by substantially increasing the number of Fellows, lengthening or making permanent the period of service, and making language training at the Foreign Service Institute available to Fellows for assignment to posts outside of their area of core linguistic ability, to ensure that nonimmigrant visa-interview wait times are not unduly affected.

Sec. 10. Visa Validity Reciprocity. The Secretary of State shall review all nonimmigrant visa reciprocity agreements and arrangements to ensure that they are, with respect to each visa classification, truly reciprocal insofar as practicable with respect to validity period and fees, as required by sections 221(c) and 281 of the INA, 8 U.S.C. 1201(c) and 1351, and other treatment. If another country does not treat United States nationals seeking nonimmigrant visas in a truly reciprocal manner, the Secretary of State shall adjust the visa validity period, fee schedule, or other treatment to match the treatment of United States nationals by that foreign country, to the extent practicable.

Sec. 11. Transparency and Data Collection. (a) To be more transparent with the American people and to implement more effectively policies and practices that serve the national interest, the Secretary of Homeland Security, in consultation with the Attorney General, shall, consistent with applicable law and national security, collect and make publicly available the following information:

(i) information regarding the number of foreign nationals in the United States who have been charged with terrorism-related offenses while in the United States; convicted of terrorism-related offenses while in the United States; or removed from the United States based on terrorism-related activity, affiliation with or provision of material support to a terrorism-related organization, or any other national-security-related reasons;

(ii) information regarding the number of foreign nationals in the United States who have been radicalized after entry into the United States and who have engaged in terrorism-related acts, or who have provided material support to terrorism-related organizations in countries that pose a threat to the United States;

(iii) information regarding the number and types of acts of gender-based violence against women, including so-called "honor killings," in the United States by foreign nationals; and

(iv) any other information relevant to public safety and security as determined by the Secretary of Homeland Security or the Attorney General, including information on the immigration status of foreign nationals charged with major offenses.

(b) The Secretary of Homeland Security shall release the initial report under subsection (a) of this section within 180 days of the effective date of this order and shall include information for the period from September 11, 2001, until the date of the initial report. Subsequent reports shall be issued every 180 days thereafter and reflect the period since the previous report.

Sec. 12. Enforcement. (a) The Secretary of State and the Secretary of Homeland Security shall consult with appropriate domestic and international partners, including countries and organizations, to ensure efficient, effective, and appropriate implementation of the actions directed in this order.

(b) In implementing this order, the Secretary of State and the Secretary of Homeland Security shall comply with all applicable laws and regulations, including, as appropriate, those providing an opportunity for individuals to claim a fear of persecution or torture, such as the credible fear determination for aliens covered by section 235(b)(1)(A) of the INA, 8 U.S.C. 1225(b)(1)(A).

(c) No immigrant or nonimmigrant visa issued before the effective date of this order shall be revoked pursuant to this order.

(d) Any individual whose visa was marked revoked or marked canceled as a result of Executive Order 13769 shall be entitled to a travel document confirming that the individual is permitted to travel to the United States and seek entry. Any prior cancellation or revocation of a visa that was solely pursuant to Executive Order 13769 shall not be the basis of inadmissibility for any future determination about entry or admissibility.

(e) This order shall not apply to an individual who has been granted asylum, to a refugee who has already been admitted to the United States, or to an individual granted withholding of removal or protection under the Convention Against Torture. Nothing in this order shall be construed to limit the ability of an individual to seek asylum, withholding of removal, or protection under the Convention Against Torture, consistent with the laws of the United States.

Sec. 13. Revocation. Executive Order 13769 of January 27, 2017, is revoked as of the effective date of this order.

Sec. 14. Effective Date. This order is effective at 12:01 a.m., eastern daylight time on March 16, 2017.

Sec. 15. Severability. (a) If any provision of this order, or the application of any provision to any person or circumstance, is held to be invalid, the remainder of this order and the application of its other provisions to any other persons or circumstances shall not be affected thereby.

(b) If any provision of this order, or the application of any provision to any person or circumstance, is held to be invalid because of the lack of certain procedural requirements, the relevant executive branch officials shall implement those procedural requirements.

Sec. 16. General Provisions. (a) Nothing in this order shall be construed to impair or otherwise affect:

(i) the authority granted by law to an executive department or agency, or the head thereof; or

(ii) the functions of the Director of the Office of Management and Budget relating to budgetary, administrative, or legislative proposals.

(b) This order shall be implemented consistent with applicable law and subject to the availability of appropriations.

(c) This order is not intended to, and does not, create any right or benefit, substantive or procedural, enforceable at law or in equity by any party against the United States, its departments, agencies, or entities, its officers, employees, or agents, or any other person.

DONALD J. TRUMP

THE WHITE HOUSE,
    March 6, 2017.

Executive Order 13769—Protecting the Nation From Foreign Terrorist Entry Into the United States January 27, 2017

EXECUTIVE ORDER = (**FIRST TRAVEL BAN**)

By the authority vested in me as President by the Constitution and laws of the United States of America, including the Immigration and Nationality Act (INA), 8 U.S.C. 1101 *et seq.*, and section 301 of title 3, United States Code, and to protect the American people from terrorist attacks by foreign nationals admitted to the United States, it is hereby ordered as follows:

Section 1. Purpose. The visa-issuance process plays a crucial role in detecting individuals with terrorist ties and stopping them from entering the United States. Perhaps in no instance was that more apparent than the terrorist attacks of September 11, 2001, when State Department policy prevented consular officers from properly scrutinizing the visa applications of several of the 19 foreign nationals who went on to murder nearly 3,000 Americans. And while the visa-issuance process was reviewed and amended after the September 11 attacks to better detect would-be terrorists from receiving visas, these measures did not stop attacks by foreign nationals who were admitted to the United States.

Numerous foreign-born individuals have been convicted or implicated in terrorism-related crimes since September 11, 2001, including foreign nationals who entered the United States after receiving visitor, student, or employment visas, or who entered through the United States refugee resettlement program. Deteriorating conditions in certain countries due to war, strife, disaster, and civil unrest increase the likelihood that terrorists will use any means possible to enter the United States. The United States must be vigilant during the visa-issuance process to ensure that those approved for admission do not intend to harm Americans and that they have no ties to terrorism.

In order to protect Americans, the United States must ensure that those admitted to this country do not bear hostile attitudes toward it and its founding principles. The United States cannot, and should not, admit those who do not support the Constitution, or those who would place violent ideologies over American law. In addition, the United States should not admit those who engage in acts of bigotry or hatred (including "honor" killings, other forms of violence against women, or the persecution of those who practice religions different from their own) or those who would oppress Americans of any race, gender, or sexual orientation.

Sec. 2. Policy. It is the policy of the United States to protect its citizens from foreign nationals who intend to commit terrorist attacks in the United States; and to prevent the admission of foreign nationals who intend to exploit United States immigration laws for malevolent purposes.

Sec. 3. Suspension of Issuance of Visas and Other Immigration Benefits to Nationals of Countries of Particular Concern. (a) The Secretary of Homeland Security, in consultation with the Secretary of State and the Director of National Intelligence, shall immediately conduct a review to determine the information needed from any country to adjudicate any visa, admission, or other benefit under the INA (adjudications) in order to determine that the individual seeking the benefit is who the individual claims to be and is not a security or public-safety threat. (b) The Secretary of Homeland Security, in consultation with the Secretary of State and the Director of National Intelligence, shall submit to the President a report on the results of the review described in subsection (a) of this section, including the Secretary of Homeland Security's determination of the information needed for adjudications and a list of countries that do not provide adequate information, within 30 days of the date of this order. The Secretary of Homeland Security shall provide a copy of the report to the Secretary of State and the Director of National Intelligence.

(c) To temporarily reduce investigative burdens on relevant agencies during the review period described in subsection (a) of this section, to ensure the proper review and maximum utilization of available resources for the screening of foreign nationals, and to ensure that adequate standards are established to prevent infiltration by foreign terrorists or criminals, pursuant to section 212(f) of the INA, 8 U.S.C. 1182(f), I hereby proclaim that the immigrant and nonimmigrant entry into the United States of aliens from countries referred to in section 217(a)(12) of the INA, 8 U.S.C. 1187(a)(12), would be detrimental to the interests of the United States, and I hereby suspend entry into the United States, as immigrants and nonimmigrants, of such persons for 90 days from the date of this order (excluding those foreign nationals traveling on diplomatic visas, North Atlantic Treaty Organization visas, C-2 visas for travel to the United Nations, and G-1, G-2, G-3, and G-4 visas).

(d) Immediately upon receipt of the report described in subsection (b) of this section regarding the information needed for adjudications, the Secretary of State shall request all foreign governments that do not supply such information to start providing such information regarding their nationals within 60 days of notification.

(e) After the 60-day period described in subsection (d) of this section expires, the Secretary of Homeland Security, in consultation with the Secretary of State, shall submit to the President a list of countries recommended for inclusion on a Presidential proclamation that would prohibit the entry of foreign nationals (excluding those foreign nationals traveling on diplomatic visas, North Atlantic Treaty Organization visas, C-2 visas for travel to the United Nations, and G-1, G-2, G-3, and G-4 visas) from countries that do not provide the information requested pursuant to subsection (d) of this section until compliance occurs.

(f) At any point after submitting the list described in subsection (e) of this section, the Secretary of State or the Secretary of Homeland Security may submit to the President the names of any additional countries recommended for similar treatment.

(g) Notwithstanding a suspension pursuant to subsection (c) of this section or pursuant to a Presidential proclamation described in subsection (e) of this section, the Secretaries of State and Homeland Security may, on a case-by-case basis, and when in the national interest, issue visas or other immigration benefits to nationals of countries for which visas and benefits are otherwise blocked.

(h) The Secretaries of State and Homeland Security shall submit to the President a joint report on the progress in implementing this order within 30 days of the date of this order, a second report within 60 days of the date of this order, a third report within 90 days of the date of this order, and a fourth report within 120 days of the date of this order.

Sec. 4. Implementing Uniform Screening Standards for All Immigration Programs. (a) The Secretary of State, the Secretary of Homeland Security, the Director of National Intelligence, and the Director of the Federal Bureau of Investigation shall implement a program, as part of the adjudication process for immigration benefits, to identify individuals seeking to enter the

United States on a fraudulent basis with the intent to cause harm, or who are at risk of causing harm subsequent to their admission. This program will include the development of a uniform screening standard and procedure, such as in-person interviews; a database of identity documents proffered by applicants to ensure that duplicate documents are not used by multiple applicants; amended application forms that include questions aimed at identifying fraudulent answers and malicious intent; a mechanism to ensure that the applicant is who the applicant claims to be; a process to evaluate the applicant's likelihood of becoming a positively contributing member of society and the applicant's ability to make contributions to the national interest; and a mechanism to assess whether or not the applicant has the intent to commit criminal or terrorist acts after entering the United States.

(b) The Secretary of Homeland Security, in conjunction with the Secretary of State, the Director of National Intelligence, and the Director of the Federal Bureau of Investigation, shall submit to the President an initial report on the progress of this directive within 60 days of the date of this order, a second report within 100 days of the date of this order, and a third report within 200 days of the date of this order.

Sec. 5. Realignment of the U.S. Refugee Admissions Program for Fiscal Year 2017. (a) The Secretary of State shall suspend the U.S. Refugee Admissions Program (USRAP) for 120 days. During the 120-day period, the Secretary of State, in conjunction with the Secretary of Homeland Security and in consultation with the Director of National Intelligence, shall review the USRAP application and adjudication process to determine what additional procedures should be taken to ensure that those approved for refugee admission do not pose a threat to the security and welfare of the United States, and shall implement such additional procedures. Refugee applicants who are already in the USRAP process may be admitted upon the initiation and completion of these revised procedures. Upon the date that is 120 days after the date of this order, the Secretary of State shall resume USRAP admissions only for nationals of countries for which the Secretary of State, the Secretary of Homeland Security, and the Director of National Intelligence have jointly determined that such additional procedures are adequate to ensure the security and welfare of the United States.

(b) Upon the resumption of USRAP admissions, the Secretary of State, in consultation with the Secretary of Homeland Security, is further directed to make changes, to the extent permitted by law, to prioritize refugee claims made by individuals on the basis of religious-based persecution, provided that the religion of the individual is a minority religion in the individual's country of nationality. Where necessary and appropriate, the Secretaries of State and Homeland Security shall recommend legislation to the President that would assist with such prioritization.

(c) Pursuant to section 212(f) of the INA, 8 U.S.C. 1182(f), I hereby proclaim that the entry of nationals of Syria as refugees is detrimental to the interests of the United States and thus suspend any such entry until such time as I have determined that sufficient changes have been made to the USRAP to ensure that admission of Syrian refugees is consistent with the national interest.

(d) Pursuant to section 212(f) of the INA, 8 U.S.C. 1182(f), I hereby proclaim that the entry of more than 50,000 refugees in fiscal year 2017 would be detrimental to the interests of the United States, and thus suspend any such entry until such time as I determine that additional admissions would be in the national interest.

(e) Notwithstanding the temporary suspension imposed pursuant to subsection (a) of this section, the Secretaries of State and Homeland Security may jointly determine to admit individuals to the United States as refugees on a case-by-case basis, in their discretion, but only so long as they determine that the admission of such individuals as refugees is in the national interest—including when the person is a religious minority in his country of nationality facing religious persecution, when admitting the person would enable the United States to conform its conduct to a preexisting international agreement, or when the person is already in transit and denying admission would cause undue hardship—and it would not pose a risk to the security or welfare of the United States.

(f) The Secretary of State shall submit to the President an initial report on the progress of the directive in subsection (b) of this section regarding prioritization of claims made by individuals on the basis of religious-based persecution within 100 days of the date of this order and shall submit a second report within 200 days of the date of this order.

(g) It is the policy of the executive branch that, to the extent permitted by law and as practicable, State and local jurisdictions be granted a role in the process of determining the placement or settlement in their jurisdictions of aliens eligible to be admitted to the United States as refugees. To that end, the Secretary of Homeland Security shall examine existing law to determine the extent to which, consistent with applicable law, State and local jurisdictions may have greater involvement in the process of determining the placement or resettlement of refugees in their jurisdictions, and shall devise a proposal to lawfully promote such involvement.

Sec. 6. Rescission of Exercise of Authority Relating to the Terrorism Grounds of Inadmissibility. The Secretaries of State and Homeland Security shall, in consultation with the Attorney General, consider rescinding the exercises of authority in section 212 of the INA, 8 U.S.C. 1182, relating to the terrorism grounds of inadmissibility, as well as any related implementing memoranda.

Sec. 7. Expedited Completion of the Biometric Entry-Exit Tracking System. (a) The Secretary of Homeland Security shall expedite the completion and implementation of a biometric entry-exit tracking system for all travelers to the United States, as recommended by the National Commission on Terrorist Attacks Upon the United States.

(b) The Secretary of Homeland Security shall submit to the President periodic reports on the progress of the directive contained in subsection (a) of this section. The initial report shall be submitted within 100 days of the date of this order, a second report shall be submitted within 200 days of the date of this order, and a third report shall be submitted within 365 days of the date of this order. Further, the Secretary shall submit a report every 180 days thereafter until the system is fully deployed and operational.

Sec. 8. Visa Interview Security. (a) The Secretary of State shall immediately suspend the Visa Interview Waiver Program and ensure compliance with section 222 of the INA, 8 U.S.C. 1202, which requires that all individuals seeking a nonimmigrant visa undergo an in-person interview, subject to specific statutory exceptions.

(b) To the extent permitted by law and subject to the availability of appropriations, the Secretary of State shall immediately expand the Consular Fellows Program, including by substantially increasing the number of Fellows, lengthening or making permanent the period of service, and making language training at the Foreign Service Institute available to Fellows for assignment to posts outside of their area of core linguistic ability, to ensure that non-immigrant visa-interview wait times are not unduly affected. *Sec. 9. Visa Validity Reciprocity.* The Secretary of State shall review all nonimmigrant visa reciprocity agreements to ensure that they are, with respect to each visa classification, truly reciprocal insofar as practicable with respect to validity period and fees, as required by sections 221(c) and 281 of the INA, 8 U.S.C. 1201(c) and 1351, and other treatment. If a country does not treat United States nationals seeking nonimmigrant visas in a reciprocal manner, the Secretary of State shall adjust the visa validity period, fee schedule, or other treatment to match the treatment of United States nationals by the foreign country, to the extent practicable.

Sec. 10. Transparency and Data Collection. (a) To be more transparent with the American people, and to more effectively implement policies and practices that serve the national interest, the Secretary of Homeland Security, in consultation with the Attorney General, shall, consistent with applicable law and national security, collect and make publicly available within 180 days, and every 180 days thereafter:

(i) information regarding the number of foreign nationals in the United States who have been charged with terrorism-related offenses while in the United States; convicted of terrorism-related offenses while in the United States; or removed from the United States based on terrorism-related activity, affiliation, or material support to a terrorism-related organization, or any other national security reasons since the date of this order or the last reporting period, whichever is later;

(ii) information regarding the number of foreign nationals in the United States who have been radicalized after entry into the United States and engaged in terrorism-related acts, or who have provided material support to terrorism-related organizations in countries that pose a threat to the United States, since the date of this order or the last reporting period, whichever is later; and

(iii) information regarding the number and types of acts of gender-based violence against women, including honor killings, in the United States by foreign nationals, since the date of this order or the last reporting period, whichever is later; and

(iv) any other information relevant to public safety and security as determined by the Secretary of Homeland Security and the Attorney General, including information on the immigration status of foreign nationals charged with major offenses.

(b) The Secretary of State shall, within one year of the date of this order, provide a report on the estimated long-term costs of the USRAP at the Federal, State, and local levels.

Sec. 11. General Provisions. (a) Nothing in this order shall be construed to impair or otherwise affect:

(i) the authority granted by law to an executive department or agency, or the head thereof; or

(ii) the functions of the Director of the Office of Management and Budget relating to budgetary, administrative, or legislative proposals.

(b) This order shall be implemented consistent with applicable law and subject to the availability of appropriations.

(c) This order is not intended to, and does not, create any right or benefit, substantive or procedural, enforceable at law or in equity by any party against the United States, its departments, agencies, or entities, its officers, employees, or agents, or any other person.

DONALD J. TRUMP

THE WHITE HOUSE,

January 27, 2017.

Memorandum on Implementing Immediate Heightened Screening and Vetting of Applications for Visas and Other Immigration Benefits
March 6, 2017

Memorandum for the Secretary of State
The Attorney General
The Secretary of Homeland Security

SUBJECT: Implementing Immediate Heightened Screening and Vetting of Applications for Visas and Other Immigration Benefits, Ensuring Enforcement of All Laws for Entry into the United States, and Increasing Transparency among Departments and Agencies of the Federal Government and for the American People

By the authority vested in me as President by the Constitution and the laws of the United States of America, including the Immigration and Nationality Act (INA), 8 U.S.C. 1101 et seq., and section 301 of title 3, United States Code, I hereby direct the following:

Section 1. Policy. It is the policy of the United States to keep its citizens safe from terrorist attacks, including those committed by foreign nationals. To avert the entry into the United States of foreign nationals who may aid, support, or commit violent, criminal, or terrorist acts, it is critical that the executive branch enhance the screening and vetting protocols and procedures for granting visas, admission to the United States, or other benefits under the INA. For that reason, in the executive order entitled, "Protecting the Nation from Foreign Terrorist Entry into the United States," and issued today, I directed the Secretary of Homeland Security, in consultation with the Secretary of State and the Director of National Intelligence, to conduct a review to "identify whether, and if so what, additional information will be needed from each foreign country to adjudicate an application by a national of that country for a visa, admission, or other benefit under the INA (adjudications) in order to determine that the individual is not a security or public-safety threat."

While that comprehensive review is ongoing, however, this Nation cannot delay the immediate implementation of additional heightened screening and vetting protocols and procedures for issuing visas to ensure that we strengthen the safety and security of our country.

Moreover, because it is my constitutional duty to "take Care that the Laws be faithfully executed," the executive branch is committed to ensuring that all laws related to entry into the United States are enforced rigorously and consistently.

Sec. 2. Enhanced Vetting Protocols and Procedures for Visas and Other Immigration Benefits. The Secretary of State and the Secretary of Homeland Security, in consultation with the Attorney General, shall, as permitted by law, implement protocols and procedures as soon as practicable that in their judgment will enhance the screening and vetting of applications for visas and all other immigration benefits, so as to increase the safety and security of the American people. These additional protocols and procedures should focus on:

(a) preventing the entry into the United States of foreign nationals who may aid, support, or commit violent, criminal, or terrorist acts; and

(b) ensuring the proper collection of all information necessary to rigorously evaluate all grounds of inadmissibility or deportability, or grounds for the denial of other immigration benefits.

Sec. 3. Enforcement of All Laws for Entry into the United States. I direct the Secretary of State, the Attorney General, the Secretary of Homeland Security, and the heads of all other relevant executive departments and agencies (as identified by the Secretary of Homeland Security) to rigorously enforce all existing grounds of inadmissibility and to ensure subsequent compliance with related laws after admission. The heads of all relevant executive departments and agencies shall issue new rules, regulations, or guidance (collectively, rules), as appropriate, to enforce laws relating to such grounds of inadmissibility and subsequent compliance. To the extent that the Secretary of Homeland Security issues such new rules, the heads of all other relevant executive departments and agencies shall, as necessary and appropriate, issue new rules that conform to them. Such new rules shall supersede any previous rules to the extent of any conflict.

Sec. 4. Transparency and Data Collection. (a) To ensure that the American people have more regular access to information, and to ensure that the executive branch shares information among its departments and agencies, the Secretary of State and Secretary of Homeland Security shall, consistent with applicable law and national security, issue regular reports regarding visas and adjustments of immigration status, written in non-technical language for broad public use and understanding. In addition to any other information released by the Secretary of State, the Attorney General, or the Secretary of Homeland Security:

(i) Beginning on April 28, 2017, and by the last day of every month thereafter, the Secretary of State shall publish the following information about actions taken during the preceding calendar month:

(A) the number of visas that have been issued from each consular office within each country during the reporting period, disaggregated by detailed visa category and country of issuance; and

(B) any other information the Secretary of State considers appropriate, including information that the Attorney General or Secretary of Homeland Security may request be published.

(ii) The Secretary of Homeland Security shall issue reports detailing the number of adjustments of immigration status that have been made during the reporting period, disaggregated by type of adjustment, type and detailed class of admission, and country of nationality. The first report shall be issued within 90 days of the date of this memorandum, and subsequent reports shall be issued every 90 days thereafter. The first report shall address data from the date of this memorandum until the report is issued, and each subsequent report shall address new data since the last report was issued.

(b) To further ensure transparency for the American people regarding the efficiency and effectiveness of our immigration programs in serving the national interest, the Secretary of State, in consultation with the Secretary of Health and Human Services, the Secretary of Homeland Security, and the Director of the Office of Management and Budget, shall, within 180 days of the date of this memorandum, submit to me a report detailing the estimated long-term costs of the United States Refugee Admissions Program at the Federal, State, and local levels, along with recommendations about how to curtail those costs.

(c) The Secretary of State, in consultation with the Director of the Office of Management and Budget, shall, within 180 days of the date of this memorandum, produce a report estimating how many refugees are being supported in countries of first asylum (near their home countries) for the same long-term cost as supporting refugees in the United States, taking into account the full lifetime cost of Federal, State, and local benefits, and the comparable cost of providing similar benefits elsewhere.

Sec. 5. General Provisions. (a) Nothing in this memorandum shall be construed to impair or otherwise affect:

(i) the authority granted by law to an executive department or agency, or the head thereof; or

(ii) the functions of the Director of the Office of Management and Budget relating to budgetary, administrative, or legislative proposals.

(b) This memorandum shall be implemented consistent with applicable law and subject to the availability of appropriations.

(c) All actions taken pursuant to this memorandum shall be consistent with requirements and authorities to protect intelligence and law enforcement sources and methods, personally identifiable information, and the confidentiality of visa records. Nothing in this memorandum shall be interpreted to supersede measures established under authority of law to protect the security and integrity of specific activities and associations that are in direct support of intelligence and law enforcement operations.

(d) This memorandum is not intended to, and does not, create any right or benefit, substantive or procedural, enforceable at law or in equity by any party against the United States, its departments, agencies, or entities, its officers, employees, or agents, or any other person.

(e) The Secretary of State is hereby authorized and directed to publish this memorandum in the Federal Register.

DONALD J. TRUMP